*In Memory of **Jihad Jule**.*

You gave me the courage to follow my dreams and make a film, a film which gave me the inspiration to write this book...

How to take your money and make a sh*t movie:

Avoiding an Indie filmmaker mistake...

Chapter 1

The Dreamer Always Dreams....Always

This is not a "how to" book. I would like to make that clear. This is a "how not to" book. As in "how not to" take $5,000 dollars and turn it into the most terribly written, edited, directed and produced piece of sh*t the short film indie market has ever seen. I will make sure that this is very obvious as we continue. However, with this being said this book can still help you make at least an interesting film. Just follow my "how not to" instructions and I can at least guarantee you will not make the same mistake I once did. When I started I thought this movie was gonna win an Oscar. Yes, you read that correctly. The same movie I destroyed in the fourth sentence of my introductory paragraph I once thought was a guaranteed trip to the academy. I even went so far as to practice my surprise acceptance speech in the shower. As well as my many surprise celebrity "oops I bumped into you, oh my I loved you in that move!" moments I was gonna plan. I made the rookie mistake of just believing in my talent to the fullest extent of disillusionment without considering what or why I should make the film. Never allow personal or selfish reasoning to justify an artistic vision.

My first mistake was securing funding before the film was even fully written. In fact the people of which I secured the funding from never even knew what the film was gonna be about until months later when the project was already finished with the editing process. Huge mistake! This should go without saying but movies need producers it's kind of a big deal. Not just to help with funding but to look at the logistics of your film and make an unbiased opinion of whether or not the story itself will sell and if so to what audience.

I made up my mind. I didn't care about the story. I was convinced that regardless of whatever mundane, melodramatic, poorly conceived and illiterate sh*t I wrote I was gonna direct the shit out of it. You see at that time I poorly over rated the directing process and horribly misjudged screen writing as well as most of the other facets of organic film making process. Lets just say your favorite director may be Quentin Tarantino, Scorsese or Spielberg for instance, not my favorites but lets run with it. ***Pulp fiction*** for instance is an amazing movie so well conceived and shot to perfection. There is a reason this film won an academy award for best screenplay and not best direction. In fact Quentin Tarantino has (as of the completion of this book) never won an Oscar for Best director but has multiple oscars for best writing. The man's written dialogue is what makes his films great, every other word is quotable especially when it comes from an always yelling Samuel L, Jackson.

Martin Scorsese finally won his first Oscar as a director with the immensely popular ***The Departed*** in 2007. This is years and years after some of his most popular and most iconic films. This is because Scorsese is one of the best actor directors in the business today. Not to be confused with Actor/Director which is an actor that also directs. He is a director that knows how to get the best performances possible out of his actors in almost every movie he has created. As an Example ***Goodfellas*** 1990, oscar nominated for best writing, best directing and best editing but oscar winner for best Actor Joe Pesci and his "Funny like what? Like I'm a clown, like i'm here for your f*cking amusement" scene. Another would be ***Taxi Driver*** 1976, Robert Di Niro's "you talkin to me" scene will go down in film history for as long as film history lasts and not because of great writing but because Bob Di Niro scarred the hell out of us..... and he add libbed the scene.

Yes, the filmmaking process is much more than just a director with his/her sexy director's hat and her/his sexy director's chair. A good film requires good screenwriting, good casting, good sets, good makeup, good location, good story boards (I can't emphasize that enough), good crafts, good crew, great production, good etcetera, great etcetera and finally a great director to put it all together and make it flow onto your screens. So much goes into a film that it seems wrong to negatively focus solely on one single aspect of what is a massive organic process. This is one of the reasons I cannot stand film critics that overemphasize cinematography in a film. One of the easiest errors to point out in a film is lighting, and wether or not the lens is in focus. So, a film critic that only emphasizes the lighting problems in a film would be just like a writing critic only detailing grammatical errors and commenting nothing substantial on the story/content. Grammar is one of the basics of writing, and thus, obviously the easiest to identify. Only an inexperienced critic focuses on grammar rather than content and story. So with this (film to book) critical comparison in mind, I have decided to take a more Jean-luc ***"Breathless"*** approach towards my grammatical carelessness. Maybe in the end the focus will be more on my story and less on the method of which I told it. My apologies if you have no idea who Godard is, or what the hell I'm even talking about right now. Let me stumble back to my original point. With only a decent director does not a decent film make. So I will fully disclose every single obstacle I approached in making my sh*t film, how I over came said obstacles and how you can avoid it all in the making of a sh*t film all of your own.

Chapter 2

Successful fundraising and how not to do it.

*If you already have secured funding or are funding the film yourself please skip this lesson and proceed to **Chapter 3**.*

I have unsuccessfully crowdfunded over nine projects, and plan to unsuccessfully crowd fund many many more. It wasn't until my eighth crowdfunding campaign that I even realized I should be adding a DETAILED description of the film to the campaign itself. Before you ask, if you haven't already learned from my heavy grammatical errors and childish scribble, yes I am that big of an idiot. That being what is, somehow I almost completely funded my Ninth film project. But I was able to successfully choke down the stretch and come up a couple thousand dollars short. Also, the site I was on was an all or nothing site meaning I lost all the donations because I didn't make my goal. Thus keeping my streak alive. Yay for me! So without further self deprecation here is how not to successfully crowd fund your film.
One of the most important things to remember is

never stop trying. If you fail on one crowdfunding site what can stop you from trying on another. Or in my case failing on another, but that's enough of that. Seriously though the only way you can guarantee your film never gets made is by giving up on it. Kickstarter, Indiegogo, go fund me, are all great user friendly sites. It's quick and easy to set a project and get it live as soon as you want. However, they leave the creativity and descriptiveness of the page up to you. So if you don't know what your doing, as I didn't, your project will come and go without many people even so much as looking at it. Take some time research your own project. Think about **ALL** of what it will take to get this film made and put that shit in your campaign. Another site Ulule was very helpful to me. They provided step by step assistance in creating and developing my fund raising campaign for optimal descriptive efficiency. It was amazing! I received constant one on one help with a person who had successfully funded so many campaigns she literally was making a career out of it. The best part it was all **FREE!** However a website such as this one can only do so much and in my case they couldn't guarantee traffic as much as the more popular crowdfunding sites. Also, Ulule was an all or nothing format and though I raised over four figures I did not receive a penny. Dreams smashed just as quickly as they once seemed realized. Sundance also offers a fantastic

fundraising service with kick starter. Sundance provides you with a professional for **FREE** to help guide you through the process of creating and funding your work. Also the lady they put me in contact with was a sweetheart and just one of the smartest, most caring and helpful people I ever had the privilege to work with.
Here are some tips to help make your crowdfunding site appear as professional as possible. Of course I say appear because let's be honest the entire business world is filled with pretend professionals that just want to make a living until they can retire or hit a jackpot. We are all just big kids. Even the one's we look up to. Anyway **<u>TIPS</u> BELOW.**

(Please excuse the format)

1. Choose a big name crowd funding site.

-This hurts newer crowdfunding websites but we gotta think about us first. The more well known the site your project is on the more likely people in your email blasts and facebook/twitter links will take your project seriously. Not to mention the amount of people that go onto this big name fundraising sites looking to become either a philanthropist or entrepreneur.

-Big name well known sites bring volume customers simple as that.

- Also I suggest choosing a non-all or nothing format for your site.

2. Create the page

- Pick your project. Have you got it....GOOD.

- This project needs to have been written. Don't just throw an idea up on a page and expect it to get money tossed at it.

- It doesn't matter what type of project you chose as long as it is something you care about and love enough to write about endlessly. The more descriptive paragraphs you can provide the better. No limit to the amount of descriptiveness you can use to create interest in your story. Go Nuts. Just remember, if it is something you don't care about yourself how do you expect to get other people to care about it?

- The About this section: Videos are your friend! Take videos of your self and describe what the funds will be used for in great detail. Make sure to keep the video under 3 minutes as to not draw the video out to longer than it needs to be. Also make sure to show excitement for your project in your speech lots of crazy hand gestures and movements, Smiles are a must. Let people like you for you but don't take the focus away from the project.

- The "what are the funds for" section: Think about everything your film may need and put it into a realistic budget. For instance all of the following usually needs money thrown at it:

$ Actors
$ Makeup,
$ locations,
$ general crew,
$ cameras,
$ camera lenses,
$ camera power cables or charging station,
$ camera memory card or film stock,
$ film editing equipment,
$ Editing Crew,
$ lighting equipment,
$ Lighting crew,
$ sound equipment,
$ Sound department,
$ Cinematographer,
$ Director
$ etc.
$ etc.
$ et...

- The more honest and descriptive you are about the way the funds will be used the more faith a potential funder will have in your production management skills. It will also bolster the faith that the film will actually be completed even if the original budget is not met. No funder will ever fund a project if they are uncertain of the projects completion. This means the more professional and honest your budget looks the more likely you are to getting a few dollars thrown your way.

- Another important topic Create Interesting REWARDS. Something tangible works far better than just handing out thank you credits and producer credits with every reward. IMDB attached or not. Send scripts as rewards. Copies of storyboards. Even offer to have someone put in the movie as an extra or dead body if they donate enough money. Be fun with your rewards. The more fun the better!

3. Before you launch

- Make a list of people you think may be interested in your project. Remember to include friends, co-workers and above all family. The most important thing to remember and what most people that have successfully crowdfunded indie projects won't tell you is that on average 30% of a successfully funded campaign comes from family and friends of the person or people starting said campaign. Of course that is just an average. Sometimes it is much lower and sometimes much higher. For instance I know a very full of himself filmmaker who brags about the large budget he crowdfunded all the time. What he conveniently leaves out is his film was "crowd"funded by only one incredibly rich relative. Hey I wont judge get that film funded how ever you can more power to you! I'm just a jealous type.

- The before launch email blast: Now that you have an entire list completed (I was told to get close to 200 names for a feature film 60 for a short) it's time to create a personalized email catered to attracting friends and family. Once you write this info soaked email send it to all the names on your list. For extra flavor add personal touches to the emails like including the person's name or even some exclusive rewards you can offer that person specifically. Have fun with it.

- Social Media: Facebook is your friend. Twitter is your friend. Instagram is also one of your many friends. Sh*t go onto E-harmony, christian mingle, black people meet and tinder and sell your film. Have no self respect just go for it, fortune favors the bold. Use all of these social media platforms to share your project. Share links. Share info. Share everything and anything you can think of and do it once a week at the most, we don't want to scare people away after all.

- Very important to remember to send these email and social media blasts at least two months before you activate your page. You want to generate flow before you start funding. Create a buzz about the date you are activating the page. Create a facebook event about the page activation and invite everybody you want. $hit send cards in the mail! Use your imagination.

4. Activate your Page

- Activating your page should be like a party. The count down has come and gone and now the day you have always waited for has finally arrived. The stage is set and ready to start filming all we need now is your money!

- After activation keep up with emails weekly to give info about how the project funding is coming along. As well as other info about the project itself, like casting, preproduction art work, pictures of locations etc. let the funders feel involved in the movie making magic.

-Don't panic if it looks like you won't make your budget. Just remember stay calm and sometimes sacrifices have to be made. Remember what Spielberg did when the animatronic shark wouldn't work while filming *Jaws.* He had to find a way to make the audience afraid of a shark that couldn't be represented by an actual shark. So he brought in the air barrels and scarred the crap out of audiences for years to come. Some say the movie might never have been as good if the shark actually worked. Sometimes necessity fuels creativity and things happen for a reason. Long story short don't be afraid of changing your original plan to fit the budget. Thats what being an indie filmmaker is all about. YOU CAN MAKE IT WORK.

Chapter 3

It's your money lose it when you need it.

Hey if you skipped the last chapter WELCOME BACK!

Kevin Smith maxed out his mother's credit cards to the tune of *thirty five thousand dollars* to make *Clerks*. This is what some businessmen would call a risky gamble. A film school drop out illegally taking money to make a film with friends in his former place of business. This happens more often than you would think. The average film student believes they can surpass the need of production and funding by just producing the movie themselves and inevitably land a sweat distribution deal. This was my mistake and it could have easily been a "mistake" for Kevin Smith as well. Kevin Smith however is way more talented than I and his 1994 film *Clerks* was destined to be an instant comedy and cult classic. If you are going to use your own money or money from family or friends hopefully you will be able to pay heed to the following chapter.

At the age of 25 I decided I was fed up with trying to sell script ideas and go ahead and start producing my own work. By producing my own work, of course, I mean robbing my parents blind. Maybe that description is a bit harsh. I used my parents unconditional love to secure funding for a film that I had not yet written and had only partially conceived. Almost absolutely throwing away what I can only hope wasn't huge chunks of their retirement money. Maybe that previous description wasn't too harsh after all. By the way 100% of the proceeds and residuals from this book will go to the victims of my stupid sh*t movie. Just to show you I'm not a complete monster. I love you Mom and Dad.

So you've got your money and you are dead set

in using it to fund your dream. One of the most important lessons I can teach you is please for the love of god set a budget and keep yourself to it. I started with a budget of only a grand. I was absolutely positive that ***one thousand dollars*** was all I would need to get my film completed the way I wanted. Before I had even started filming my budget had ballooned to over double that estimate. By the time filming completed (which was only three days I might add) I was ***five thousand dollars*** in the hole. Make a list of things you will need to complete your film and force yourself into your budget. Do not make adjustments as you go along. You will get blinded by shiny new things you do not need and equipment you may not even use.

Lets start with equipment rentals. What I initially wanted was to make a film with a nice affordable HD camera. Nothing to fancy just enough so my film can be watched on a big screen and not have static and fuzz everywhere. What I had in mind was a canon 5Di Digital SLSR which at the time would have been more than enough to film with and would only have cost $170 for the entire three day shoot. However, when I got on the rental website a shiny new camera caught my eye. It was a magnificent 4k shooting scarlet red dragon camera that would only cost $500 per day to shoot with. Easily worth the money I thought. Then I realized they only give you the brain of the camera for that much, lenses, power cables, a 4k hd tv screen to see what your filming with, handles just for holding the camera, batteries, memory cards and memory card converters were all sold separately. All in all just to get the camera to work brought the entire rental price up to $1000 a day by itself. A *thirty five thousand* dollar camera renting at about a *thousand* dollars a day. Doesn't take a genius to see that business for what it's worth. Im just glad I didn't try to buy the camera like Tommy Wiseau did when making *The Room*. Cameras depreciate in value within a year, unless you are gonna rent them out never buy one. By the time my 4k film came out a year later 5k was already the shiny next new thing.

Next we will look at renting equipment you never needed in the first place. I was the biggest and dumbest mark this rental company ever landed. So I can't really say this enough, make a storyboard and find out the equipment you need to make your vision become a reality. Don't just come up with everything at the last minute like I did. I rented a Steadicam rig for around $190 a day and really only used it for one shot. Which ended up being one of the poorest lit and shakiest shot scenes in the entire film I might add. Also I rented extra lenses and attachments I never used that all in all added $300 dollars to my end budget. I was going at this movie will all heart and no brain. My execution was not one of professional preparedness but that of an overexcited child that just bought/rented a plethora of new toys to play with.

I ran into three problems financially with the cast and crew. On one end I ended up falling for the big time producer facade, I desperately wanted the professionals I hired to know I meant business and that I was a legit filmmaker. Obviously I was no where near the talented professional I pretended to be. On the other end I am an extremely friendly person who cares too much about what people think of me. I ended up either over paying supporting cast and crew because of my extreme friendliness or because of my over inflated professional ego. Those two problems were bad and they fueled each other during the entire shoot but the biggest problem was the third and most unforgivable of all. I had talked friends of mine into doing the film for free, yes for free, even though I had promised them compensation beforehand. I took advantage of friends and family to get this sh*tty film made and even though I am still very close with everyone involved I will never be able to forgive myself for this.

Location was a big problem for me as well. Not that I couldn't find a place I wanted to film in, I just could not control my now hot air ballon sized ego from tearing apart my wallet. I wanted to spend $400 a day to shoot in an elaborate bar/club. I would have to pay the bar for shutting down a section of its club for 2 days. Luckily for me a friend who worked at a bar in town was able to hook me up with a great place that already had a section shut down for pending restoration. I was able to get the filming location for around $100 a day. I was not so lucky with the apartment I needed to rent which I dropped almost $300 total on. That my friends is how you finish a film five times over your initial estimated budget so word to the wise, don't do that.

Chapter 4

Don't get Sued, people love to sue.

Unless your name is William Friedkin and your movie is *The French Connection* I would strongly suggest you follow the law of the land and get permits to film in certain locations. As well as making sure every actor you have on the camera contractually allows you to use their likeness in the film. If not you could lose the money you paid them to be in the film and then later if the film takes off they could sue you for a percentage of the film itself if not all of it. Finding out the information you need to make your shoot legal is very easy and can be found with one google search. In fact there are free templates made by very awesome indie film fans that can be used as all your film contracts. Again most of it is free just make sure you look up what you need to do to make your project legit and get it done.

Actor Release form. Find a template for these and print out as many as you can. From there you only need to enter the name of your production and producers as well as the signature and name of the actor involved and bingo your done. At the end of this chapter I will include pdfs versions of templates I used as examples of what to looks for. Minors are a different problem altogether. You need to have the written consent of the parent or legal guardian as well as the minor and all signatures involved therein on a MINOR TALENT RELEASE statement.

Also make sure to acquire rental insurance on any expensive item you rent. You don't want to accidentally break that *thirty five thousand* dollar camera trying to put it back in its box. Get the insurance it might seem like an extra budgetary hassle but it is well worth the risk involved. The insurance will cover damage during production, during shipping and will also cover the equipment if its been shipped to you broken. I actually received a $150 a day lens broken and was told I had to pay for it because it left them unbroken, however I had attained insurance before renting and not only was everything covered I also received my money back.

Below are some examples of forms you may need.

TALENT RELEASE FORM

I authorize the undersigned Producer to make use of my appearance on:
PROGRAM TITLE:

_____

_____
PRODUCER'S NAME:

_____

_____
PRODUCER'S PHONE NUMBER:

_____

DATE OF TAPING:

_____

_____ I understand that I am to receive no compensation for this appearance.

The Producer shall have complete ownership of the program. I give the Producer the right to use my name, likeness and biographical material to publicize the program and the services of the Producer.

The Producer may:

1. Photograph me and record my voice and likeness for the purpose of the production mentioned above, whether by film, videotape, magnetic tape, digitally or otherwise;

2. Make copies of the photographs and recordings so made;

3. Use my name and likeness for the purposes of education, promotion or advertising of the sale or trading in the photographs, recordings and any copies so made. I further understand the master tape remains the property of the Producer and that there will be no

restrictions on the number of times that my name and likeness may be used.

Name (please print)_____
_____ Date: _____

Address
_____
_____

City
_____
__ State _____ Zip Code
_____

Talent Signature (Parent or Guardian if under 18 years of age)

_____
_____ Date:
_____

LOCATION RELEASE FORM

I, the undersigned hereby grant permission to _____ the right to enter and remain upon _____ (the Property), which shall include not only real property but any fixtures, equipment or other personal property thereat or thereon, located at _____, with personnel and equipment (including without limitations, props, temporary sets, lighting, camera and special effects equipment) for the purpose of photographing scenes and making recordings of said Property in connection with the production of a digital media text on the following date(s): _____.

This permission includes the right to take motion pictures, videotapes, still photographs and/or sound recordings on and of any and all portions of the Property and all names associated there with or which appear in, on or about the Property.

This permission also grants all rights of every nature whatsoever in and to all films and photographs taken and recordings made hereunder, including without limitation of all copyrights therein and renewals and extensions thereof, and the exclusive right to reproduce, exhibit, distribute, and otherwise exploit in perpetuity throughout the universe (in whole or in part) such films, photographs and recordings in any and all media, whether now known or hereafter devised, including without limitation in and in connection with the documentary video and the advertising and other exploitation thereof.

I certify that I have the full right and authority to enter into this agreement and grant the rights herein granted, and that the consent or permission of no other person, firm, or entity is necessary in order to enable you to exercise or enjoy the rights herein granted.

ACCEPTED & AGREED TO: NAME (please print) ADDRESS

_____

_____
_____
_____
_____

SIGNATURE

_____
_____ DATE
_____

Chapter 5

Seriously who needs to storyboard?

<u>Failing to prepare is preparing to fail</u>

I think I mentioned earlier that I hadn't really written a script yet when I received funding for my idea. Let me explain this further by going into some detail. By this point I had written in my little phone note pad over 100 ideas for films, poems and other things. I always got really excited about the latest one so excited in fact I could write about it for days. Kinda like the idea for writing this book. Anyway the idea I decided to fund was just the latest idea I had and was most excited about, but the idea itself was only one scene. So I needed to hunker down and write an entire script around this one scene before my set film date, which was within the month. Obviously this is just asking for trouble.

This Ignorance of mine continued to occur throughout the making of the film. I set a date for the film and delivery of the equipment before I even really secured the locations. Luckily I ended up securing the bar for the already scheduled date. That really could have been a waste of up to about two grand. I also never fully created a storyboard and instead went with a shooting script that had no shot direction on it what so ever. The shooting script contained only lines of dialogue and other scenes I wanted to cover for that day. So all the angles, all the lighting, all the cinematography was all done off the cuff while in the process shooting the movie.

While filming I thought this method was actually working. As the day went on however I got more and more bogged down with the sheer amount of shooting I needed done. Eventually my shots became more and more simplistic until finally the shots became just completely bland with basic lighting. I don't have to tell you how the film turned out. I tried to edit the film for months and months after I got the final footage just to try an fix lighting and color issues. Finally I decided to give up and just render most of the footage to black and white. Thank god I got that 4k camera am I right? All that money went straight into a high definition black and white poorly shot obvious student film. You listening Academy?

I actually believed I was gonna submit this thing to Sundance hoping the academy would appreciate some inner genius I had. I'll get back to that later. The lack of preparation didn't give me enough time to get creative with my story. Unfortunately some of us may only get one shot like this to make a film. I probably blew the only opportunity I will ever have like this again. I can tell you as a filmmaker who has made eight films since this one. I wish I could take back that story I decided to shoot with, I wish I would've gone for a better story and would've tried not to rush the film out as much as I did. You got to set yourself up for success the best you can. If you never fully give yourself a chance to be at your best people will believe what they are seeing is your best. The only thing I do now is completely own my project. I loved the people I worked on it with they worked there @sses of and at the end of the day I feel I let them all down. Don't forget to just give yourself a chance to succeed.

Chapter 6

The film's personality: Who's in it?

Casting, one of the few things I think I did right.

This will be a tricky chapter for me to write. Up until now I've tried to be as impartial as possible without being to obvious as to what film of mine I'm actually talking about. I don't want to be too specific because I would really hate to hurt anyone's feelings. For some of the people involved it's the biggest role they have ever had in a film. I don't want to diminish what the film meant to me personally. It is honestly something I would never replace in the world. I was able to film with friends and also made new life long friends along the way. It was honestly one of the most positive experiences in my life and every time I see anyone involved I'm instantly happier. Just makes me sad the film is no good. Anyway I sent out a post on a Louisiana actors face book page of the people I needed and waited to get responses.

Casting went on for about a month. I want to also clarify that in this chapter I will be not only describing my casting choices for characters but also the crew choices as well. It's tough to try and film in the south with a small indie crew and budget. When you come up to somebody in Louisiana and try to get them in a realistic dramatic film that involves relationships and connections, most of them immediately assume porn. Some people that would be the first question. Do I need to kiss someone? I would say, yes. They would hang up on me immediately or block me. Never even asked to look at the script. It was rough.

The lead male actor was easy for me to get, he

was a good friend of mine and still is. He is a fantastic actor, very professional and always excited to act, I love the guy. Every other role was much much harder. They would ask do I have to kiss? And send me a picture of the guy? Before I knew it half the replies to the casting notifications had withdrawn without meeting in person or even asking for the script. People would see me and assume porn, guess I got one of those Burt Reynolds in *Boogie Nights* auras. Like I had a vision for a porno with a heart and decent love story. RIP to Burt, I loved him in everything he ever did. Gonna miss you Gator. My script had some interesting personality with it, meaning I needed a specific type of actor. This was really hard to find in Baton Rouge. Maybe New Orleans would have been much easier to film in and find willing talent. In fact the female lead and one of the supporting roles came from New Orleans to help. The angels traveled an hour to get to set and after filming would drive the hour back. No questions asked ever. When I finally got all of the roles filled I jumped the gun and decided to schedule the rental equipment. Obviously I over looked the fact that I did not have a complete crew. I knew that I would be handling the camera, as I always do unless I'm also acting in the film, but I hadn't found any sound or lighting guys. As luck would have it a friend of mine that I

worked with previously had done recording before, he just didn't have any sound equipment. I worked out a deal with him because as you know if you have made a film before sound can get very labor intensive. Especially the editing process which I completely screwed over for this poor guy, but I'll get more into that in the next chapter.
So I now have a sound guy, but I still needed someone who could handle the lighting equipment as well as handle the memory cards for the cameras, the basic stand in roles for some actors, prop situation, a translator and makeup. I made arrangements with multiple people some would accept and later decline upon seeing the script. Others would hear what was being offered monetarily for the position accept it and later decline when I suggested the possibility of longer than eight hour work nights. Honestly it is a good thing that those guys backed out because none of my shoots were under eight hours in fact one of the shoots was fifteen hours long. If you are in the film industry you know to expect between twelve to sixteen hour work days. It is very common in this line of work.
Three weeks before the filming I'm talking to a friend of mine freaking out lets just say his name is Blake. Im telling him that i'm getting really pressed for time because all of this

equipment is coming in and I have nobody who can help me set it up. Well let me give you some quick back story on Blake. Blake was the kinda guy the worked on a favor system. If you did him a big favor he would do any favor you needed in return no questions asked. It just so happened that Blake had driven all the way to Texas (about a four hour drive) before realizing he left his wallet at a friends house. When he called me to ask if I could pick up the wallet I told him "no problem, then I realized the friend who's house he left the wallet in was with him in Texas. So I ended up having to break into this man's house while being watched closely by the neighbors. Eventually I found the wallet and met him half way. Blake never forgot that and offered to help with the film no problem. Poor Blake ended up doing more than just setting up the lights. He also ended up handling the memory cards for the cameras, did the basic stand in roles for some actors and did the prop situation. As well as being an all around best boy. I would later help him move out every bit of furniture he had in his apartment to his new house, no questions asked. I knew after the fifteen hour day I owed him a big one. Fortunately one of my actors hooked me up with a translator. So now that I had the other positions filled the only thing I was needing was a makeup artist. Nothing spectacular just someone to do basic makeup and help the actors get camera ready. Someone I went to school with actually answered the crew notice and I hired her immediately.

It took me two weeks before the expected shooting date to realize that I was gonna have three actors acting in what was essentially an empty bar. I hadn't even had a casting call for extras yet. I set up a casting call that day explaining how many people I needed and where the filming location was. Of course if I was just now thinking about the possible need for extras what chance was it that I worked in an extras budget into the film? I got zero hits on the first few casting calls that claimed "no pay". Then a stroke of genius hit me offer up to three free drinks a person as compensation for having to come to the set and stay that length of time. Within minutes I got seven hits. Doesn't matter who you are I guess, a free drink is a free drink. The night of the shoot came and call time for crew came and went. The makeup artist never showed. Again I went into full on panic mode. I had already mentioned the fact I didn't set up any shots or a storyboard before hand. I had no idea how I was gonna have to handle the lighting for this 4k camera to not abuse my actors. In steps my lead actor friend, being the consummate professional he always is had makeup ready and with him just in case of such an issue. This was huge as the male actors were the only problem for makeup to begin with. So he handled the make up for himself and one of the other actors.

Up to the night of the shoot I was still not getting solid confirmation on who would be appearing as extras for me. When I walked onto set I had no clue wether or not a single extra was gonna show for me. Sometimes it is better to be lucky than good, and sometimes it's better to be a bit of both. I decided to push back the extra heavy scenes I was gonna need and just shot the primary actors in their specific scenes. Once I finished those scenes like clock work the extras flowed in one by one. I was able to get every extra in and out within two hours. Some didn't want to leave.

Can you imagine the amount of headache I would've spared myself had I prepared a little better? Or had I consorted and actual producer on the needs I wasn't thinking about at the time. Even something as simple as giving myself more time to work before getting over zealous and just jumping straight into a shooting date. It pays off big time in the long run just to be able to look at something objectively for a second. Not everything has to be rushed all the time. I should have showed my film it's due diligence. I'm lucky to have gotten through the hiring process with a team in tact.

Chapter 7

Ready. Steady. Action.

Wait. What's my motivation?

Game time, the filming date was tomorrow and my shiny new 4k toy had just come in. I opened it up with my new DP/Best boy/lighting tech/everything else Blake. He was just as excited as I was. We were ready to start filming with this thirty five thousand dollar camera. The red scarlet dragon was actually a fairly simple set up. Nothing really too extreme needed to be prepared. One of the few problems we had with the set up was getting the Steadicam to work correctly. We really didn't have the time it needed to commit to figuring it out so we basically just winged it. Hence the extra shaky and terrible Steadicam sequences in the finished film. I would later find out that this would be indicative of the entire shoot.

We get to the bar the day before to try and mess

with some lighting and angles. We basically started a last ditch effort to story board and attempt some type of makeshift plan. The bar was open to us for only a couple of hours that night as they knew they needed to be open for at least 8 hours for us the following day. Little did we know that thanks to the absence of the makeup artist the next day all the planed shots and lighting angles would need to be thrown out. Altered for the less professional makeup we ended up having to roll with. Of course that is not a slight on my lead actor who came in the clutch with his own makeup. It's just that makeup is not the way he earns his living and we had expected a veteran.

We picked up all of the equipment and Blake and threw it into the back of a silver ford F-150. I had decided to fill one of the extra roles my self as nobody wanted to fill it. So I was dressed in a servers uniform all black long sleeves and long dress pants. In case you didn't know Louisiana can get pretty hot. On this particular day it had reached 93 degrees and extremely humid. The F-150 was the only vehicle we had available big enough to carry all the equipment and unfortunately for me the air conditioning was out. Rolling down the window in Louisiana while driving is not a desirable prospect the humid air holds the heat. So much so that the wind comes in hot and heavy and won't cool you off as much as make matters worse.

We finally got to set. Blake and I took everything we had out of the back of the truck and hoisted it up the stairs and into the bar. By now I was drenched with sweat and ready to get things under way. I sat In the bar with my audio specialist enjoying the central air while I could. Because I knew the air conditioning was too loud and was gonna need to be shut off. The bar had black out windows so we really didn't need to wait till the sun went down to film the night scene. But we also didn't want to sit in a black tented hot box and bake in the sun as well as under multiple hot set lights. It wouldn't take long before the entire cast and crew would be begging for the sweet release of night. But, knowing we were struggling for time and that we had an unlimited supply of water available to us on site, we shut of the AC and went at it.

This is around the time the extras didn't show. In fact they wouldn't show until the sun finally did go down. Which as this time of year was pretty late. So I decided to take advantage and shoot all my scenes with the primary actors. Can I tell you that was one of the most uncomfortable scenes I have ever attempted to film in my life. My behind the camera replacement kept moving the camera and messing up shots I had framed. The unfortunate actors and myself were sitting in heavily layered clothing waiting to get just the first shot right. It almost took an hour to get it the way I wanted it. This might have been me just being a bit of a pre madona director, but stop changing the framing man. Finally we finished the scene (which didn't make the final cut anyway) and I was mercifully able to get out of my layered clothing.

I choose not to celebrate too loudly, the other actors still had to finish their scenes under direct spot light and the sun was still not scheduled to go down for another couple hours. I could finally put on my directors hat and get back behind the camera where I felt comfortable. The next few shots were all close up shots. Tiny little intermediary shots to help with editing later as well as dramatic timing. We fired these shots off very quickly getting most of them done within the hour. This gave us exactly another hour to real off as many of the scenes with the primary actors as we could. I shot every one of these on a tripod in the bar. With all of the last minute arrangements I had to make off the cuff, this is when I started to jeopardize my artistic vision. I would film the dialogue and reaction all from one angle for each actor knowing I would just edit it seamlessly. I did this from three different angles to try to get some variety in the shots. Alas, it was not enough in the finished project these scenes are very stagnant and boring. Which is very unfortunate because the acting I was getting was very, very good. I did not do them justice at all. It wasn't until I started post production that I realized my male and female actors (the two main actors in the entire scene) never shared the screen together. No over the shoulder shots, no transitions or movements involving them both. Just plain steady medium shots, nothing special, and never what I had intended.

The sun went down, the weather chilled and the extras came and went. The scenes that followed we were able to get out in almost a cookie cutter fashion. Every line of dialogue was said while being filmed from four different angles. We did one actor first then the second and finally the third who we only shot from two angles. It was getting close to the end of the night and we were behind pace thanks to the very first scene we shot that night. Again we never used it. I decided to try and keep everyone as late as I could. I felt terrible because I knew some of the actors still had to get to New Orleans that night. Going through a 12 hour shoot and then drive 70 minutes in

solid darkness, most of which is on a bridge over lake Pontchartrain.
No thanks.

Remember earlier when I referenced me putting my audio tech in a tough spot. The 4k camera does not record straight into the brain. So the shots we take with the camera are mute and the audio has to be edited over it in post. Well here we are wrapping up the first night of filming and the poor audio tech realizes I haven't yet called out any shots to mark what scene, dialogue or shot he was supposed to be recording. Meaning he was going to have to go back over every single recording and listen for dialogue or some kind of que as to what should have been where. A lot of it was going to have to involve guessing as most of the shots were silent ones. This being what it was he did a fantastic f*ckin job. He set up a system that helped me exponentially during editing but probably took him days and days of non stop work to get prepared. Like I said all my fault and I still owe him so much more.
Well as nice as my sound expert was he didn't want to bother me knowing how busy I was. So I never had a chance to fix the problem for the ENTIRE shoot but I think he started to tag them himself while I was preparing shots. He knew that I was swamped and took it upon himself

not to even bother me with the problem. I would work with this guy again tomorrow if I could. Not to mention that his sense of humor was amazing and mirrored mine and the rest of the cast and crew perfectly.

By day two we realized how lucky we all really were to be working with each other. Every person on the set was hilarious. Never a dull moment with any of these guys and it was really sad it was only gonna be another day and a half shoot. The Run for day 2 was incredibly simple compared to the hectic planning of day 1. Just had to clean up what was left of the day 1 shoots which was really only half a scene and then prepare for the long tracking shots and the outdoor shots. This day was easy and by far one of the most fun. I didn't even mind that most of the night I was strapped with a relativity heavy Steadicam. I had embraced the shoot and with the availability of some free time I was able to become creative again with my shot selection. So I spent a good portion of the scenes adding to the script here and there as well as preparing for day 3 in the next set. I think because of this the second half of the film in the apartment set has much better shot selections and also flows better.

However day three would still have it's share of problems. I would start off slow that day since we arrived during day time, so I tried to set up the night time shoots as much as I could. The sheer volume of takes that was gonna be needed in the climax of the film scared the crap out of me. I knew I had to get it done that day, and the fact that the scene had to be shot at night didn't help me in the time restrictions department. Also, if I did not mention this before the entire scene would be done in a language I did not know fluently. This would become a headache for me later in postproduction. Again I never marked my shots or the audio during the entire production. What an extreme rookie mistake.

Day three started early on a Sunday morning. I knew it was gonna be a hard, long day as we only had the set for one day. We as a team flourished under the pressure. We found the scenes that could be shot during the day and knocked them out quickly. We were both productive and having fun. This is how I wanted the entire shoot to go. We were all inspiring one another to do better jobs with only our attitudes and our humor. These are the days I would never change. As the day turned into night and got really late some of the actors started taking naps while I filmed around their scenes. The next day their day jobs were looming and here we are 1 am just 12 hours into the shoot. We would finally finish the day 3 hours later at 4am. My poor actors would

have to drive an hour back to New Orleans just in time for rush hour morning traffic and they also had day jobs. But everyone was sad to see it end especially Blake and myself. It took three days but we had made friends for life. I also would later figure out that in my rushed state on day 1 and 3 I completely forgot to film an entire scene. Reshoots were on the horizon.
I did myself no favors cutting corners during production. You never want to rush art, it jeopardizes artistic vision. I know that kinda makes me sound like an artsy director in a fight with his money crazed all business producer, but I honestly believe it to be true. The first day was my fault and it turned out to be detrimental to the film as a whole, no matter how the second and third days shooting went. If I had just planned that first day better maybe the film would be more appreciated by its director today. Every now and then I desperately want to start cutting it again, just to try and make it something decent for everyone who was involved to appreciate and feel proud to be a part of.

Chapter 8

Reshoots

I chose big font because, this is how overblown the reshoots here for me.

I had actually only one scene I needed to have done from the original script. But because I desperately wanted to make up for some of the terrible dailies I had seen, I decided to add multiple additional scenes to the finished film. These were to be filmed with a cheap cannon t3i which would end up becoming my sole filming utensil for the next few years to come. I rigged the camera itself to get some beautiful shots out of it and man did I.
I decided to take a supporting character and kind of follow him to the bar. I quickly turned this character from extra to supporting to almost one of the leads. He didn't mind and we could film when ever we felt like it, always guerrilla style where ever we wanted. He was and is my uncle and one of the funniest people I've ever had the pleasure to be around. He was in a wheel chair at the time but never let it stop

his attitude. I enlisted the help of another good friend of mine this one was also extremely talented but in a very different way from Blake. He and I ended up adding and additional 20+ shots with over 50 total takes within the few days following initial shooting. We had wheelchair shots all over the place. We rigged tracking shots real amateurish guerrilla style stuff with a skateboard and a wooden board to skate it across. It would follow the wheels of the chair.

I became completely blind to the original vision of my film. At one point I flirted with the prospect of making the wheelchair bound man the main Lead actor. It was going to have a deep but brisk stale humor with an inner monologue. Yes this coupled with the fact I already decided to grey scale pretty much the entire film meant a complete tonal shift from quirky romantic comedy with a twist to some kind of Neo noir voyeuristic wheelchair bound vagrant story. Putting it mildly, I had lost my way trying to make this film work.

Once I finished the saga of Gianni nubs Arsonetti aka the guy in the wheel chair, I started meeting up to begin recording voice overs. Some of the audio was just plain missing, again no doubt it was my fault. So we called up some of our big actors and started reshooting audio in a studio. We recorded over

70 old and new lines of dialogue including yells, grunts, groans and other human sounds. Then I went back to nubs (wheelchair) and started recording inner monologue and things he could be saying under his breath. I came out of the recordings with Nubs with over 6 hours of continuous non stop ad libbing. The guy was a riot, he had improvised most of the work but kept it close to what I was trying to envision. It got to the point where professionalism went out the window and I started asking for people to just record certain lines of dialogue with their phones and send it to me. I no longer cared about the hum un filtered audio can pick up. I just wanted to make this film work in any way I possibly could. If that meant having to rewrite the entire script then so be it. I was determined.

Finally we were able to get to the last legitimate scene needed for the original vision. The one take and only thing I really needed before the word "reshoots" set me off on a tangent that led to completely rewriting the script and adding new crucial characters with inner monologues. The shoot called for one thing and one thing alone the lead female actor just needed to be shot taking her wedding ring off in the bathroom. This was by far the easiest thing I have ever shot in my entire career. It took two takes and all of twenty five minutes to get right, she nailed it on the first take . I just wanted to film it again incase I missed something in the first one. I was now finally able to put the filming and recording of this dream turned nightmare to bed. Focusing on the new task at hand – editing.

Chapter 9

Editing – The never ending process

By now I was so deliriously happy I finished filming I didn't even consider how tough the next task at hand was even going to be. Little did I know that with the addition of my day job the first watchable version of my film was not going to be finished for another three months. Even that version was edited and re-edited. The final version was finished some 2 years after filming and I might change it up again. Lets start from the beginning of the editing process. It took two 12 hour days just to go through every bit of footage, name and catalog it. I hadn't even had time to think about the audio which couldn't possibly sync no matter how hard I'd try. This editing process was destined to be a mad continuos battle with me in a dark room for 10-12 hours a day almost every day for three months.

The first few days were actually the easiest. Believe it or not editing is one of my favorite things to do. I enjoy creation don't get me wrong but for some reason the editing of two shots to create a story just makes me happy. I was like one of those crazy people that enjoy putting together ten thousand piece puzzles. I was putting together a giant organic puzzle that did not yet have a finished image to work toward. Every individual frame offered a new opportunity when added to another. Every line spoken differently when edited to another response created a deferent context. The conversation changed from the previous edit and because of the two tones it went from a conversation with possibly sexual over tones to one of possible stress due to marital tension. The thought of creating through editing has always been the reason I enjoy filmmaking. Even when I was younger, around 11, I would edit anything I could. Of course at that age it was mostly highlight reels and other things like that. But one day in sixth grade I heard about a class project for eighth graders that I was going to have to complete before I could finish middle school. The subject was create a presentation about World War 2, you could have a power point or even create a video. Well thats all I needed to know. I decided to work on it immediately. Within three days I had created a 15 minute documentary about the invasion of normandy leading into the American and Russian discovery of the Holocaust. I had also added (because I was 12 or 13 at the time) Linkin park and NightWish to the documentary as back ground music and had it perfectly edited to the films transitions. I was only in sixth grade but I could tell I had finished something great.

I remember trying to find anyway I could to edit on what ever program I could find. For the world war 2 documentary I actually used powerpoint with video additions. I attached music and videos to slides and used it as my editing software. I got really good at editing this way and started editing anything I could. I enjoyed it so much, for me this was the end all be all of existence. It wasn't until I was in high school that I got my hands on windows movie maker. From here I created possibly 40 college football highlight reels until I went to college and discovered what final cut was all about. I have now edited up to 20 projects on final cut. I'm always editing.

It took almost a month to get all of the audio synced up to the paired 4k video. By this time I was physically and emotionally drained. I had to do all of the work of editing without being able to actually splice two pieces of film together. But now that the audio was ready the only thing standing in my way was deciding which version to start editing first. The original romantic comedy vision with a twist or the dark neo noir vagrant monologue film. In my exhausted stupor I decided to do them both and create one long film.

Making this version of the movie presented me with multiple problems. Most of the shots I had with Nubs in the wheelchair are the first shots in the film. The movie would open up with this wheelchair bound vagrant wheeling across a parking lot with an inner monologue about things he has seen in his travels. Now that I think about it, it was such a horrible idea. I can't help but laugh. My uncle was very good, he was not the problem. The problem was the first five minutes of the film are a slow paced building suspense feel with a deep voice in the background and black and white visuals in the rain. Then the original movie begins which is way more up tempo at the beginning with immediate lite comedy.

I'll set some pace for you. Shot one dark screen flashes into a dark rainy empty parking lot. Rolling onto screen from camera left is nubs, his squeaky wheel the only audio besides the pitter patter of rain, not a soul in the lot except him. Cut to shot two another angle of the wheelchair in the parking lot. This is a long shot showing the sheer amount of distance this vagrant will have to cover just to try to get where he is going. It is this long shot where the inner monologue begins.

Nubs: "It was cold and rainy"

A nice bleak descriptive statement to get the COMEDY film started. God it is hard to watch today.

Nubs: "Im so use to it I barely notice the rain any more"

He covers a little bit of distance and cut to shot three monologue over a tire spinning by itself, this is the aforementioned guerrilla tracking shot with the t3i tied to a skateboard.

Nubs: "I've seen quite a lot of things in my time but what I will see tonight.

Nubs pauses as he gets lost in thought thinking about that night

Nubs: "is nothing that special really"

Nubs pauses again as if confused

Nubs: "But hell. What else was going on that night?"

I tried to throw in some lite comedy with the bleakness. I was possibly gonna add some additional lines here like.

Nubs: "Now that I think of it, it was a really boring night"

I hadn't considered at the time the fact that Nubs is no where in the third act of the film. So how exactly was I supposed to explain this character's knowledge of the events that take place?

Nubs: "Oh well I already started, I guess I'll tell this story any way."

Looking back at it, it is quite a shame that I paced it so poorly because the shots are really quite beautiful for such a cheap camera. Finally we have another long shot this time an extreme long shot. Showing the entire building the bar is in. The bar is not a stand alone building it is in a strip mall. This wouldn't be the first time I filmed in a location like this. The extreme long shot is on a tripod, all the movement is on the screen. We see Nubs wheel in from screen left slowly making his way to the front stair case of the bar. This is where the first tonal shift and pacing problem occurred. The dark first few minutes were now about to seamlessly transition into the faster paced comedy of the original vision. He is slowly making his way to the bar he has wheeled about half way to it. Finally he approaches the front, only a staircase between him and the bar. He looks around see's no ramps and turns around his back facing the staircase.

Nubs: "Why do these places never have ramps?"

Nubs pauses as he looks around

Nubs: "shouldn't it be a law by now"?

He looks up the staircase and back down

Nubs: "well I already came this far"

He wheels up to the staircase backwards the inner monologue is over now, he is touching the bottom of the stairs with the back of his wheelchair. Slowly he looks around and boom quick tonal shift he starts going up the staircase backwards. He wheels one step at a time slow at first then quick until he stops close to the top and looks dead at the camera breaking the

fourth wall. Cut to the opening title.
I thought this was brilliant when I first edited it. How could this not be good I thought, it goes from slow grumpy pace to extremely childish almost Benny Hill pace. Set up the rest of the film perfectly. Boy, was I kidding myself. That scene would be the most childish and have the quickest tempo out of every other scene in the rest of the film. In fact the film slows down to a snails pace in the bar, not five minutes from the staircase traversing.
Now that I had the introductory scene out of the way we could cut to the actual point of the film. When I sat in my editing room and watched the finished product of that very first day of filming my heart sank. It was so intensely boring. The shots with me in it were on a huge very steady tripod but the guy behind the camera was still trying to move the framing. So i'm watching the scene and I realized the camera keeps moving, not in a slow barely recognizable way of course. It was jerking around very obviously. I lost it, the scene was not extremely important but it was a set up for later in the film. Now it had to be cut and left on the floor.
Now I love this guy, he is today a very very close friend of mine. To this day I still have no clue what he was trying to do. He actually came up to me a couple months after filming, after I had seen what he did to the shot of course, and

asked if he would receive a directors credit. A directors credit? For holding the camera and pointing it in the frame that I set up, and you couldn't even do that right. Again, I love the dude but damn that was rough not to take out all my frustration on him verbally. I just nodded my head, told him that's not really what a director does and sent him on his way.

After I trashed my big scene I moved onto the next problem at hand. The bland cookie cutter tripod shots that are supposed to introduce the two main characters not only to the audience but to each other. He is supposed to spot her in the bar and walk over and talk to her , and they are supposed to have a delicate romance blossoming scene together. Some how I thought I had achieved this even though they do not share the screen once through the entire scene. In fact through the entire bar sequence they only share the screen twice. When he first see's her approach the bar and when they are having a "romantic" moment at the end. Even the back and forth with the bartender is hard to watch. It's just back and forth medium shots of the two men saying their dialogue until the scene ends. Looking back at it there are so many shot selections and ideas I want to add to the film. For instance there is a scene where the female lead writes a note to the male lead. So in my haste I decided to film her writing a note from

above looking down at the note. It's a really bland shot that I'm obviously not proud of at all. Instead I would've liked to shoot a low angle shot from the side of the bar getting the writing of the note at the bottom of the screen and in the background facing the camera is the lead actor staring at the note. I would even shift focus from the note to the male lead, hold for a second and cut to the next shot of her passing it to him.
I could fill an entire book with things I could've done differently to make the

film better. I might not have gone with the techno music as the film's background. I might not have spent so much time doing reshoots. I probably would have casted differently for specific things.
I wouldn't have spent so much on the camera, knowing I was going to alter the footage to black and white. Or I could just get a cheaper camera and hire a professional cinematographer to help take the weight off my shoulders. The biggest problem was having to waste 3 months getting the footage to successfully sync up with the audio, neither of which were labeled effectively.
Editing the apartment scene became one of the toughest projects I have ever worked as an editor and director. I faced multiple problems.

First and foremost I was unable to get access to the set before the shooting date. Which means the entire set design, decoration, color selection, shot selection and sound proofing all had to be done the same day we filmed. What this means is the end scenes are very bland in color and shot selection. Yet another reason to want to greyscale the entire project. I was only able to add in a couple of last second shots as well as transitional shots that I liked. Most of the rest of the day was just trying to get the filming done.

Another problem was again the audio issue. The audio clips had been tagged by count for this scene however the entire scene was in another language. So listening to the clips I couldn't tell what was being said. Even better most of the audio was silent with a lot of the scene using heavy sighs, claps and hand gestures. So in this was the problem. How on earth was I to edit a scene when I the only things to go on are an occasional sigh or loud hand gesture. I would watch one shot and listen to 80-90 tapes of audio just to find out what synched with what. It was a nightmare. I spent almost an entire week on 10 shots all of the same scene, 2 of which didn't even make it to the final version of the film.

Remember the film was in another language. I did not speak this language, and I was the only person editing the film. I desperately needed an interpreter because I had no idea what shot was the beginning of the scene, what shot was the middle and what was the end. At first, I was only able to work with the shots I understood. I tried for about a week to edit the sequence myself. I bought a book to help me learn the basics of the language, and pieced together words I had looked up with words from the script and finally match them to what I was seeing in the clip. It was incredibly time consuming.

After a while I gave up on trying to do it all myself and enlisted the help of my actors as well as a translator. I had to start sending them videos of the footage via text message. I would send them piece by piece footage whenever they weren't working and they would get back to me with what the scene was as soon as they could. Of course while I was waiting on them I would still try to translate other footage by myself. When I say this project took three months to edit, I mean it took three months of non-stop work to finally get it all done.

It did finally get done. It took a week of filming two months of editing and an additional month editing it back and forth into different story lines. You know, editing from my original vision to the vision I reshot it to be and back. Including the additional edits to the color scheme of the film. Mostly back and forth from color to black and white. Even after I submitted the films the first time I continued to edit like this another two years. I guess you could say my need to make the film work became kind of an obsession.

I wish I considered all of these problems when I first started working on this project. I could have easily fixed the problems with the foreign language scenes by simple organization. I could have identically labeled every shot with every audio clip and then follow up mark it in the script accordingly. It could have been as easy as counting it down. Unfortunately I had absolutely all vision and no knowledge of production management.

A simple hollywood clapboard and audible mark was all I needed. Boom, that would have fixed two months of editing changing a five month project into a three month film. It would have also provided me more time to submit to film festivals, especially since the late editing process made me miss various festival deadlines. It wouldn't stop me from trying however, but then again nothing could. I had just spent almost half a year on this beast, I needed some closure. Who knows maybe my disasterpiece would be officially selected after all.

CHAPTER 10

Submitting to the right Festival, And what that means.

This project became more than just telling a story and my vision. This project became my only opportunity in life to do what I loved, what I've always wanted to do. It was always a dream of mine to work on all things film. It didn't matter to me if I was directing and producing my own projects or just working as an extra. I loved being on set, I loved to learn as much as I could. One day hoping to get invited to one of those big named film festivals. Walk down the red carpet and talk about my vision and why the story mattered to me personally. Now I finally had my opportunity to submit something of my own. I was afraid on my first attempt I had fumbled the ball and it was gonna be all over.

I learned a lot in school but what most film schools don't tell you is they can only teach you the basics. Basic screenwriting, basic editing, basic whatever. Everything is intro level, even the advanced classes. The only way you could really learn is by watching film, observing on set yourself and making your own projects. This is because every crew, production and cast work differently, no one structured template can work for everything. Filmmaking is an organic process and if anyone tells you differently then they just haven't had enough experience to know differently.

The end project may look like your storyboard sure but by the time it's completed it something very different. One actor can create a different type of character than another it's rare to find one character that multiple actors can do very well, for instance the joker and Blofeld. But, even those characters can give actors like two time oscar winner Christoph Waltz and oscar winner Jared Leto problems. Some actors are just better suited for certain characters than others. It's not only the on camera things that are constantly changing but behind the scenes as well. Some directors look forward to onset inspirational changes. David lynch for instance works most of his on set inspiration into his films, if he doesn't get the opportunity he feels he and the film have been robbed.

Film festivals are not an area I knew much about. As far as I was concerned you made a great film and magically everyone important would see it. First thing I wanted to do was submit to vimeo and youtube, to try and extend visibility as much as possible. Weeks went by without so much as a single view on any streaming service. Finally I decided to look around at some of the more prestigious festivals, Telluride, Cannes, Slamdance, Sundance etc. I was looking for any and every type of festival I could find. Yet, I still had no clue how to get into them. Google is a magnificent tool for the unprepared. Just simply type in "how do I submit my film to film festivals?"and a plethora of opportunities

present themselves.
I recognized the name of one of the sites immediately, withoutabox. I saw it at the bottom of almost every film festival website I looked into. As far as I could tell it was the only film festival submittal site there was. I signed up to withoutabox as soon as I could, and made a profile, it was all free and easy. Of course once I got the key to submitting I went crazy. This of course is where things can get expensive because the best festivals are far from cheap to submit to. Sundance at it's most affordable was around $45 to submit a short film. I think a feature film submittal is close to $70. Now, $45 to $70 is nothing when you are sitting on a budget of over hundreds of thousands of dollars. You would be surprised what some of these "indie" projects are actually made for. It almost feels like this should be divided into three categories not just two, Hollywood mega movies, Indie films and broke ass visionary films. As the later, later $45-$60 per festival was way to expensive for me, I would need to make this more than just a hobby.
I must have submitted to 10+ international film festivals that year. I just assumed I was going to get selected to whatever festival I wanted to get into. I didn't even consider the politics behind these things. Most of these film festivals will

focus on the always obvious production value while judging. They will usually only let in a film, if the production value is not there, if this film speaks to political opinions of the festival. What this means is a film that looks like lower value about a father that loses his son is less likely to make it in than a lower value film about police violence. Some film festivals will only accept certain types of film makers. Like a women only festival, native american only festival, african american only festival and so on. Some festivals will allow all types of filmmakers but show their hands by having specific awards for best films by a woman, african american or etc. I was actually emailed by a festival some years later and told they wanted to include my film, then they asked me what "ethnicity" I was and reascended the offer when they found out I was a caucasian male. This wasn't indicative of all or even most festivals but it was still happening. It was getting to the point where a caucasian lower class american male with a shitty film had no hope of selection.

I looked up the most expensive and exclusive festivals and just assumed my shit was gonna get in. Of course looking at the situation now I can't blame any film festival for not accepting my film. The film was beyond terrible at that first edit and only a moderately understandable film after the final edit. The first edit was twice as long as the final film. I still had not decided which story I wanted to tell with the film and instead used both the original vision and the added on extra bullshit. Seven minutes of a guy wheeling himself around a parking lot and rambling to himself. Followed by a couple minutes of the main character talking to his wife about her infidelity. Then cut back to the man in the wheelchair trying to wheel up a set of stairs backwards. By itself that shot was funny added in with the tone of the film it was distracting and made zero sense. Not to mention the tone shifts to a different style of comedy once the actual story started, which wasn't until the 7 minute mark.

Remember the greatest directors take suggestions but only use them if they match the theme or tone of the film. Indiana Jones was to be in a massive sword fight lasting several minutes. Steven Spielberg was excited and had the entire fight mapped out and choreographed. Then Harrison Ford shows up the day of the shoot with the flu. He does a couple walk throughs of the fight and even gets it on film a couple times. But, on the next take Harrison decides to do something different, he talks to the director and the stunt man he fights with. They begin rolling cameras, the crowd parts, the man starts wielding both of his swords and in a moment of sheer brilliance Indiana remembers he has a pistol and shoots the man dead. It was cinematic gold, a nice meta look at the tropes of most action films as well as a well timed joke that matched the films tone and humor perfectly.

One of the great experiences of being a shitty independent film maker is you get to literally pay for your own rejection. I spent the following year being rejected from every film festival I submitted to. Even some deaf film festivals wanted nothing to do with my work. I was untouchable month after month more and more rejection followed by me trying to edit and re-edit the film. Unsure of what the problem was and clinging like a bird on a wire to my dream. Had I realized the problems I have already stated with my film I could've saved my self lots of money. All in all I spent close to $400 submitting to a minimum of 50 film festivals that I had no need to submit to. I was blinded by the amount of time I spent on the film. I could not see it's flaws because I was so close to it.

The year went by and I slowly went back to my day job. Every now and then I would collect a couple of ideas together and start re-editing what I was working on. I had no interest in my day job yet I was very good at it. I would end up spending a lot of time at work thinking about new ways to edit certain scenes. Maybe even think about new scenes to film and add to the movie. As more and more time went by I started to realize that I missed my chance. The final notification dates for the last film festivals on my list, my last hopes of being a nationally selected indie film maker, came and went. Every response the same.

Mr. Thomas we appreciate you submitting your fine film to our festival. We regret to inform you that though your film shows obvious talent we have no available room to show your film in our festival. We appreciate you giving us your money and hope that you make the same mistake again next year. BLAH Blah blah blah blah, blah blah.

Sincerely,
That festival you desperately wanted to get into.

Maybe the universe was trying to tell me that this wasn't for me. I already had a child, maybe it was time for me to grow up and stop being a dreamer. Take some responsibility and crush those hopes and dreams I clung too. Be an adult and realize that what you want is too unrealistic. Go back to school and find a job you could be good at without hating yourself. Find something that doesn't make you want to rip your hair from your scalp and that preferably pays you well. Do that job until you die and have regrets your whole life for never giving it a really good shot. Teach your children the same thing. Have a dream kids then when you grow up become an engineer. My apologies if you grew up wanting to be an engineer, there is no problem with that I can tell you, that is a great dream to have as a kid. After the film festival dream was squandered I went back to the editing room and cut out every inch of the man in the wheelchair from the opening. I was not going to allow my dream to end. Instead I had decided to publish the films to Youtube at least this way people would be able to watch it if they wanted to. I had no problems with the public giving opinions of my film. I just did not like watching people watch my films. As long as they did it by themselves I was fine.

A couple more months went by and I was starting to see a new girl. She was amazing, probably one of the more supportive people (without being related to) I have ever met. At this point in time I had already stopped pursuing film festivals and stopped editing my film. My future it seemed did not involve what I was most interested in. Until one night when she forced me to show it to her. I explained to her before hand that it wasn't really that good. She didn't want to hear it the only thing she was interested in was watching the film. Most people that watched it had more critical things to say, of course to that point it was mostly film producers and film makers who had seen it. I made her watch it in the other room while I dreaded the future conversation. The film ended, she came out of the back room and looked at me.

"I like it" she said. "Why aren't you more proud of it?"

I had no idea what to say. I had expected the same film criticisms I had heard the last few months. But, instead she asks why are you not proud of it. I tried to explain to her the flaws I saw in the film, the extra footage I kept adding and deleting, the editing process. She listened to me as I couldn't help but make every excuse possible for why I disliked my own film. Then when I had finished she said very calmly.

"You are over thinking everything" She said

I tried to interrupt her but she continued.

"You created something. You wrote the script,

you put the actors in it, you coached them and you filmed it. You pieced it together and even edited it to music. You worked through the language barriers with your actors. You didn't let the fact that you couldn't understand what was being said stop you in your editing process. You had a story to tell and you told it wonderfully."

She paused and looked at me.

"What does it matter what anyone else thinks?"

She was right. Her words hit me like an emotional dump truck. I had spent so much time trying to make this film into something it wasn't, something I thought other people would like. Instead of the movie I would like to see. So what the film wasn't "***Casablanca***"or "***Amadeus***"it was never intended to be. This was the indie filmmaker equivalent of *"Studio interference"* and my film had become a cheaper version of "***Suicide Squad"***. From that moment on I never took my own work for granted again. I made sure that what I edited was what I initially had planned and nothing more.
I went back and edited my film the way I had initially planned. I brought out the old script and re-edited it frame by frame scene by scene.

It took me about a month to fully get the film right. By the time it was finished most of my uncle's part in the movie was trashed. Sure he was upset but when he saw the finished film he realized why I had done it. This go around I had no intention of submitting it to any film festivals. Wether this film was festival worthy no longer mattered to me. I posted the finished edit on to Youtube and went on with my life. A few more months went by and we reached the year anniversary of the making of the film. The film still unreleased anywhere accept youtube and vimeo. I had not thought about the movie again until one of my actresses approached me. She asked me why I hadn't tried submitting the film to any festivals. I decided to be honest with her, I told her I had and we were rejected from every single one. She took my honesty and ran with it. She gave me a slew of "don't give up" and "you are really very talented" one liners. Eventually I caved and told her I would submit to another film festival. But, this time I would let the actors tell me the one's they wanted to submit to. It occurred to me that these deaf actors would know more about deaf film festivals than I obviously would. She sent me two festivals both of them international. One was a festival in Los Angeles the other a huge festival in Seattle.

"Here we go again" I thought.

I went onto a new submission service called Film Freeway and submitted to both film festivals. The notification dates were still a very long ways away so I would have to wait longer this time for rejection. I will never forget when it happened. I was in the super dome in New Orleans, Louisiana. I was at a concert with my girlfriend and her family. Before the concert started our group tried to venture to the upper deck areas of the stadium. We were stopped by a nice looking gentleman holding tickets. He looked at us and said where are you sitting. We handed him our tickets and showed him we were in the upper deck. He shook his head.

"Guess my favorite color" he asked.

We said "Blue"

He shook his head violently "Wrong" and shrugged.

He handed us the tickets back. He had switched out our tickets with some new ones. These were down on the floor. In the front row closest to the stage. I had never been that lucky in my life I thought, but it seems my luck was not yet over. Before the concert started I left to get some drinks in the new private concessions stand that only people with good floor seats can get into. While I was waiting for my order my phone buzzed. I looked down at it and saw I had a new email. I opened it. It was from film freeway, it read as follows.

*Congratulations The strength within you film festival in Los Angeles California has changed your submission to **Selected.** You will be emailed information by the festival soon in regards to putting together your film's press package.*

I Started to cry. Looking back at it now it what such as small thing but it didn't matter. In that moment all of my hard work instantly paid off. To this day getting into a film festival is more important to me than winning any prizes the festival has to offer. Just the ability to say that I was nominated for something. Something I did was recognized by panel and selected to show at their event. It will always mean more to me than judging.

This selection was truly the effort of the support of many people. I would never have been able to get the film done the way it needed to be if not for so many. It is truly one of the

most blessed experiences of my life and I will never exchange it for anything. I alerted my cast and crew that we made it to a festival in Los Angeles. We all decided we had to go. This was something that we could talk about the rest of our lives and we did it together. Regardless of how big the festival was this was an accomplishment for our selves. It gave us validation for our hard work.
We traveled to Los Angeles in November. Having lived in the south my whole life and never really traveling much I had no idea what to expect. We rented a room in the Roosevelt hotel in Hollywood right across the street from the legendary Chinese theatre. It was an amazing experience and one I hope to do again in my lifetime. The film festival was two days so we stayed in hollywood for an entire week. We did the tourist thing then went to the festival that weekend. The film didn't win any awards but I did get to make some new life long friends as well as speak on the directors panel.

I got a bit ahead of my self. In November we went to this film festival, we were selected in August. After the initial selection I went on a film maker spree. I decided I no longer cared what people thought of the work and decided to make things I wanted to see. By October I had already filmed three short horror film projects, a music video and ***Body Language***. I was on a role, by the time the November festival swung around I had 20+ selections for every film I had created. The best part, every film was a project I was able to do with friends. It was a fantastic streak that has not yet ended.

In the following year I would go on to make 5 more short films and secure funding for a feature. I have not yet made it to the upper echelon of a Sundance or Cannes but I can honestly say I am happy. As of this book I have written and/or produced/published over 20 films. My films *"**Body Language**", "**Newborn**", "**Tresspass**", "**Lucas**", "**Vessel/Greed**", "**Baton Rouge summer of 2016**"* and *"**Salem Waiting**"* can all be found on Amazon Prime as well as various other streaming services. If this teaches you anything Never give up on a dream.

Chapter 11
IN CONCLUSION

...The point of this little book

I could have easily never pursued my dream. I would be sitting at a desk working a job I really do not care for and telling myself it's all ok. In fairness I'm not making a million dollars a year. But, I am making money doing what I love and that my friends is the definition of a dream job. The entire point of this book is to help you not make a terrible film. I hope as an indie film maker you take all this advice and run with it. But, do not be afraid to make a film.
Sure I directed my first film at the age of 26, but I have been writing and creating since I was a teenager. I believe everyone who has a creative idea has done the same thing I'm about to describe. You want to sit on that idea until you have enough
1. Money

2. Time
3. resources
4. etc

to do that idea as much justice as possible. The problem Is the idea of a perfect creation. No such things exist. If you wait till you can do your project as much justice as possible it may never get done. In fact many people I know have great ideas they never try to attempt because they are busy. They are afraid to dilute the idea by rushing it out or doing it with a cheaper budget. I'm here to tell you that you can always do the project over again with more money. Do a cheaper version of it now, get it out there. If you don't it may never get done. James Wan had an idea for a horror movie. He did not have the money to create the film he wanted. Instead he created a version he could afford to do and called it ***Saw.*** Eventually this short film became a feature length multi million dollar franchise. But if James Wan waited until he could make the feature and never made the short we probably would never have the ***Conjuring***, ***Saw*** or ***Annabelle*** movies. Many directors have made their films into short projects first and have created a career because of them. Another example is Damien Chazelle. He created a short project called ***Whiplash*** which turned into a multiple academy award winning feature film. He also directed the super successful film *LA LA Land.*

This is a <u>how not to</u>book, but it is also a <u>how to</u>book. As in, how to not regret never having tried. You don't really know until you've given it your all. Even then the only person that can stop you trying is yourself. Never be afraid to attempt your dreams. It doesn't have to be film it could be anything. At the very least give it a shot. You never know, you may just surprise yourself.

www.ingramcontent.com/pod-product-compliance
Lightning Source LLC
Chambersburg PA
CBHW030449220526
45464CB00006B/2462